Citizenship and PSHE
Book 3

Contents

Deena Haydon
Pat King
Christine Moorcroft

What personal qualities are these children showing?

1. Copy and complete the table.

Child	Qualities
a	
b	

2. What might the children have said and done if they did not have these personal qualities?

Words for personal qualities

bravery
cleverness
determination
generosity
honesty
humour
kindness
loyalty
modesty
patience
perseverance
sympathy
unselfishness

Some people are admired by others.

3. List the reasons why other children might admire Bhavna in this poem.

What are Bhavna's personal qualities?

My friend Bhavna

In Bhavna's hair is a three-ribboned braid.
She can plait it in seconds without any aid.
She can write with both hands – and with her feet.
But she never tries to make it neat.

If you ask her to play skipping, she may say 'yes',
Then persuade you to play her at chess.
She plays in goal wearing a bright green hat,
And saved six penalties – but said nothing of that.

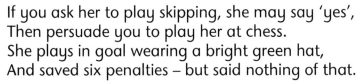

4. What do you admire about your friends?

5. What do you think others admire about you? Ask them.

6. Imagine an important visitor is coming to your school. A guide is needed. Write a short speech (about 60 words) to explain why you should be chosen to be the guide.

Think about how they treat others, how they act in groups, what they can do … .

It is the start of a new school year.
The children have made 'New Year resolutions'.

 1. Why do you think each child has made that particular resolution?

What might help them to keep their resolutions?

Copy and complete the table.

What are the children like now? What do they want to be like?

Name	Reason for resolution	What might help him or her
Charlotte		

People make resolutions because they want to change in some way.

2. Talk to a partner about a way in which you want to change.

Write your 'New Year resolution'.
It will be your goal.

Ask a partner to help you keep it.

Learn something new.

Develop a personal quality.

Develop a skill.

Give up a bad habit.

Start a new habit.

My New Year resolution

I shall achieve this by the end of the school year.

signed

witnessed by

3. List the things you will do to reach your goal.

List anything that might make it difficult to reach your goal.

What could you do about these difficulties?

No more than four sweets today.

I have not lost my temper.

Mon.	Tues.	Wed.
✓	✓	✗

Thur.	Fri.	Sat.	Sun.
✓	✓	✓	✓

Don't rush. Keep it neat!

COUNT TO TEN IF YOU FEEL ANGRY OR IMPATIENT.

I have not bitten my nails today.

M	T	W	T	F	S	S
✓	✓	✓	✗	✓	✓	✗

Have you PRACTISED today?

Everyone makes mistakes.
Sometimes mistakes can help us to do better.

1. What mistakes did Robert and Alice make?
What might each of them have learned?

2. Talk to a partner about
mistakes you have made.

Think about different kinds
of mistakes: school work, things
you shouldn't have said or done, or things
you have forgotten.

3. List some of your mistakes.
Did you learn from them or
did you repeat them?

Copy and complete the table.

Mistake	Learned from	Repeated

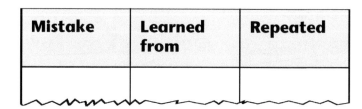

How have your
mistakes changed your
behaviour?

4. Write about a mistake from which you have learned.
What did you learn?

What mistakes have these children made?

5. What could each child have learned from his or her mistake?

6. Do they accept responsibility for their mistakes?
   Talk to a partner about what each child could do in future.

7. Write a letter to one of the children.
   Explain how he or she could learn from his or her mistake.

People can experience many different feelings in a short time.

1. How did Kelly feel in each picture?
How can you tell?
Why did she feel like this?
Copy and complete the table.

As well as thinking of words like 'anger' for feelings, think about what was going through Kelly's mind.

Picture	Kelly's feelings	How I can tell	Why she felt like this
a			
b			

2. Talk to a partner about how Kelly's mum might have felt in pictures **b**, **c** and **d**.

How might Kelly's actions have affected her mum's feelings?

3. Kelly could have expressed her feelings in different ways.

With a partner, list all the ways in which Kelly could have expressed her feelings in each picture.

How might Kelly's actions be helping her to cope with her feelings?

picture a
Dance for joy.

picture b
Go for a walk.

picture c
Sulk in her bedroom.

picture d
Write a note to say 'sorry'.

4. During the week, make a note of any times when you have strong emotions.

Describe how you expressed them.

You could compare your notes with those of a friend.

I was jealous when my mum bought my sister some new trainers. I shouted and wrote mean things about her.

Like everyone, young people approaching puberty sometimes have strong emotions.

1. Talk to a partner about the emotions that the children are feeling.

   Write an explanation for why each child acts as he or she does.

2. With a partner, write your ideas about what else they could have done.

   List some ideas to help one of the children cope with the situation that he or she does not like.

3. The situations in the pictures are quite common.

How can people prepare for them?

Puberty is a time of change. It can make small worries big.

If you are nervous, tell yourself, 'I <u>can</u> do it.' Take slow, deep breaths. Count to ten. Then try again.

Worries can affect people's emotions and behaviour.

4. What do you think are the main things that worry ten-year-olds?

With a partner, list these worries.

School work, clothes, people laughing ... .

... being told off, being bullied.

Share your list with your group.

5. Choose one worry.

Write what you think would help someone to handle his or her feelings of concern.
What could he or she do to overcome the worry?

Right and wrong

| Monday afternoon | Monday afternoon | Tuesday morning |

Speech bubbles:
- "I wonder where Kylie is. She should be home by now."
- "Just tell your dad you missed the bus."
- "Hi Ben. How's Kylie? I saw her in town yesterday."

citizenship

1. Discuss, with a partner, what is happening in each picture.
How do you think Kylie's father and Kylie feel?
What do you think might happen when Kylie gets home on Tuesday afternoon?
Why do you think Kylie lied to her father?

2. Why do people sometimes not tell the truth?
Copy and complete the list.

> *Sometimes people do not tell the truth because:*
> *1. they do not want to get into trouble*
> *2. they ... .*

Think about feelings and emotions, the consequences, and other people's reactions.

3. What is the difference between 'lie' and 'fib'?
Write a definition of each word; using an example may help.

Copy and complete the table.

Lie means	Fib means
e.g.	e.g.

12

4. Find out what **tactful** and **diplomatic** mean.
Explain the meanings in your own words.
In groups, make some 'Tact is …' or 'Diplomacy is …' cards for display.

It cost a fortune. Do you like it?

Diplomacy is saying, 'I don't agree with you, but I understand why you feel like that.'

Tact is changing the subject when you can see someone is getting annoyed.

I don't like it at all. Should I tell her?

5. Do you think Lucca should tell Sophie what he thinks?
How might Sophie feel if Lucca is honest?
Can you think of a tactful answer?

I love the colour!

It's not the sort of thing I'd wear but it looks great on you!

6. Think about a time when you have had to be tactful.
Describe the situation, what you did or said and why, to a partner.

Think about:
● other people's feelings or reactions
● the consequences
● loyalty.

Have you ever told a 'half-truth'? Why?
Think of three reasons for not telling the whole truth.

Is it always wise to tell the whole truth?

Antisocial behaviour

 1. What is happening in this picture?

Write a story to show the conversation the four friends might have had in the few minutes before this incident.

 Draw each boy with a thought bubble.
What might each be thinking?

Think about positive thoughts and feelings and negative thoughts and feelings.
Do you think they all feel the same?
Why are they doing this?

2. In a group, share your ideas about what the boys were thinking.
Discuss with your group what might happen next.
Think of different possibilities.
For each one decide who would be affected. Think of as many consequences as possible.

The people in the house might phone the police, then … .

The fire brigade might come and a fire officer might be injured. Their families would be worried.

Setting fire to property deliberately is the crime of **arson**.

3. List examples of antisocial behaviour in the picture. What might be the consequences of each antisocial act?

Think about the consequences for the person who did it and for other people.

4. Why do people behave in antisocial ways?

Responsibilities in the family

1. What responsibilities does Joel have at home?

2. Make a list of the responsibilities you have in your family.
Compare your list with those of three other children.
Are they similar?

Think about:
- caring for people
- looking after pets
- jobs around the house
- taking care of yourself and your things ... .

3. Note all the jobs that are done in your household.
On your list, record who in your family does each job.
How often is each job carried out?
Copy and complete the table:

Job	Who does it	How often
cooking vacuuming dusting gardening washing clothes	Mum, Ron Lucy me	daily weekly

In what ways does the range of responsibilities surprise you?
How are they shared?
Could you do more?

4. Parents or carers have some responsibility for looking after you. You have some responsibility for taking care of yourself and letting them know you are safe and well.
In what ways do you do this?
Copy and complete the speech bubbles.

Think about:
● what you need to tell them
● why they need to know
● what may happen if you don't tell the truth or change your plans.

Services

Public services are services people need.

1. List the services provided in this community.

Welfare	Communication	Transport
social services welfare office	telephone Internet cafe	railway

Think about: health, welfare, transport, education, work, leisure, energy, finance, communication and waste.

Copy and complete the table.

2. What services are provided in your local community?
Who uses these services?
During what times are they available?

Copy and complete the table.

Type of service	Who is it for?	When is it provided?	How is it paid for?
bus service	everyone	Mon–Sat 8am–7pm	taxes and fares
meals on wheels			

Find out how the services are paid for. For example, are they paid for with people's taxes?
Do people pay for them when they use them?
Do voluntary groups provide them?

3. Some services are needed by everyone.
Some are needed by groups with particular needs.

Make a table showing necessary services and services needed by:
1. older people
2. parents with children under five
3. teenagers
4. people with physical disabilities or learning disorders.

Services needed by everyone	Services needed by parents with children under five
Health service Electricity	Crêches

Local democracy

In some schools, pupils are involved in decision-making as members of a school council.

Each class votes for someone who will speak on their behalf – their class representative.

The class representatives meet with members of staff to talk about important school issues and to make decisions.

1. What qualities do you think a class representative needs?
Draw a picture of the Ideal Class Representative.

understanding

organised

fair

good listener

respects other people's opinions

thinks before speaking

Think about:
- personal qualities
- reactions to others
- communication skills
- ability to negotiate and compromise.

2. Can anyone learn to develop these qualities?
What can you do to practise the skills or develop the qualities needed to represent a group?

3. Who makes decisions on behalf of your local community? How are these people chosen? With a partner, devise a set of questions to help you investigate the role of a local **councillor**.

Think about: how they are chosen, on whose behalf they work, what they do, how decisions are made, where decisions are made.

Word bank

chair	proposal
committee	representative
council	resolution
debate	secretary
election	treasurer
policy	vote

4. Find out about national decision-making.
Write a short paragraph about two of the following:

Parliament   Political party   Opposition
Government   Prime minister   Manifesto

How can you make sure that your views are represented by people acting on your behalf?

Debating environmental issues

Human activities sometimes damage the environment.

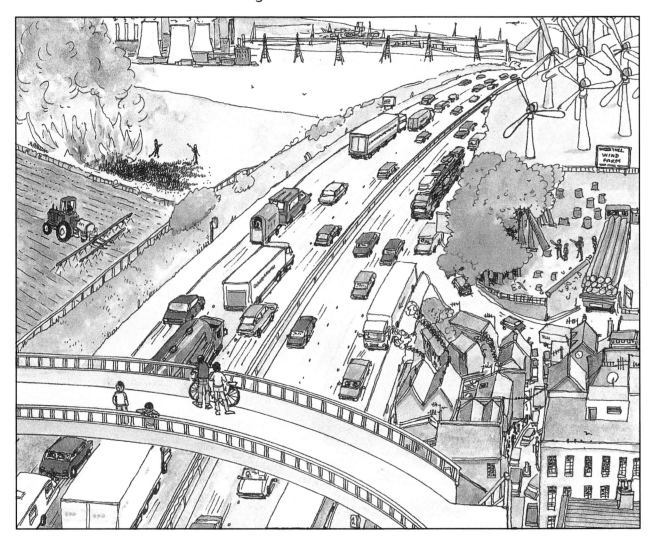

 1. How is the environment being damaged in the picture?

Continue the table.
Add some other things that damage the environment.

Damage to the environment	
air	land

 2. Find something in the picture that is used to make electricity without polluting the environment.
How is this a good solution?
Who might disagree? Why?

3. Why do people do things that harm the environment? Discuss the benefits and harmful consequences.
Copy and complete the table.

Activity	Reason
spraying crops	+ to kill pests - pollutes water
using cars	+ to get from one place to another quickly

4. Find out more about something that damages the environment.

Global warming

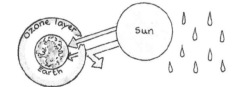

The ozone layer   Acid rain

Waste disposal

Pesticides and weedkillers

Radiation

Transport

Sewage

5. Who is responsible for the environment?
Explain your answer.

6. What can people do to stop the environment being damaged? Add your own ideas and complete the table.

Think about: energy, water, waste, transport.

Looking after the environment	
Transport	Walk as much as possible – leave the car behind.
Waste	Recycle bottles, cans, paper and plastic items.
Farming	Use fewer pesticides.

What could you do to help the world environment?

Clean choices

These are what Peter uses to keep himself clean.

These are what Lesley uses to keep herself clean.

1. Describe how Peter and Lesley might keep their bodies clean.

2. As you grow and change, your body has different **hygiene** needs.

Draw a body outline. Mark the parts that need extra washing and care as you grow up.

3. What would happen if Peter and Lesley did not keep their bodies clean?

4. Find out what happens when bacteria breed on
- the skin
- the teeth
- the hair.

Copy and complete the table.

What might Peter and Lesley do each morning and evening to keep themselves clean?

Part of the body	Result of poor hygiene
teeth	decay, bad breath

Lifestyle

People from different times have had different ways of keeping clean.
People nowadays have different ways of keeping clean.

The Ancient Romans rubbed oil into their skin and scraped it off, along with any dirt, using a strigil.

Akate lives in Ghana. He uses a chewing-stick to clean his teeth.

Clare cleans her face with cleansing cream.

5. Find out about other ways in which people keep their skin, teeth and hair clean.

Choose one of these that you find most interesting.

6. With a partner, prepare a presentation about this method of keeping clean.

Use CD-ROM reference material and the Internet.

Your presentation could be a promotion.

Harmful substances

You have a choice about some of the substances that enter your body.

| Fresh air | Fruit | Water |
| Alcohol | Bread | Cigarette smoke |

1. Which substances would you choose to put into your body?

Explain your answers.

Copy and continue the table.

Substance	Would/would not choose it (✓or ✗)	Reason
fruit		

Add two other substances you would choose to put into your body and two you would not.

A drug is a chemical that alters how the body works.
Drugs can be helpful, as medicines, or they can be harmful.
Some people take drugs when they are not ill.
They use the drug to alter their state of mind or how they feel.
This can harm their bodies and their minds.

2. What drugs do you know about that people use? How do they use them? Copy and complete the table.

drug	How people use it			
	smoke	sniff	swallow	inject
nicotine (cigarettes)				

You may know people who use alcohol and cigarettes as drugs.

I had better not drive. That's six pints I've had – I think I'll have a few more.

We'll walk home – I'll have another couple of glasses of wine and then we'll go.

3. Describe how alcohol might affect the people in the picture. What foolish decisions have the people made? What sensible decision have they made?

Cigarettes can also harm people.
Most people know about the harm but some people still choose to smoke.

4. Carry out a survey to find out:
a. why people started smoking
b. why they don't stop.

5. Make up an advertising jingle to persuade people either not to smoke or to drink less alcohol.

Playing safe

In this story Salim and Hasana make choices.

Salim switched off his computer and looked out of the window. The rain had stopped. "Hasana," he said to his sister, "I'm fed up with being indoors and sitting still, are you?"

"Yes. Let's phone Simon and Faye to play cricket. Jason might come, too."

In the kitchen, their mother and father were busy peeling and chopping fruit. "May we phone Simon and Faye to see if they can come and play cricket with us in the field?" asked Salim. Dad looked at his watch with one eye and at Mum with the other. Salim and Hasana saw 'OK' on Mum's face. "That's a good idea," said Dad.

Hasana had already pressed the automatic dial key for Simon and Faye's number: "Oh, good. Yes, we'll bring them; you bring the wickets. See you in ten minutes."

"It's two o'clock now," said Dad. "Come back by four. Have a good game."

Faye was setting up the wickets when they got to the field. Hasana asked if they should play further over, away from the road. "Yes," said the others, "if we play here we'll keep hitting the ball on to the road."

"Not if I'm fielding," laughed Simon. They all laughed, but they moved the wickets.

Another boy and girl were playing ball nearby. "May we play?" asked the girl, adding, "There's a proper pitch over at the sports ground, with much smoother grass; why don't we play there?"

"That's a good idea," said Salim. The others agreed, and off they went. They had never been there before. It was the best game they had ever played. They didn't stop until it was too dark to see the ball.

---

1. List the choices that Salim and Hasana had to make.

2. In which of their decisions did Salim and Hasana avoid risks? How?
In which decisions did they take risks?

What were the risks?
Explain how they acted responsibly or irresponsibly.

Think about the choices they <u>could</u> have made.

Rachel and her mother have a choice of two routes to walk from home to school:

| The main road | The footpath |

Think about traffic and people.

3. With a partner, discuss the safety and the risks in each route.

Copy and complete the table.

Route	Safety	Risks
a		
b		

4. Which route should they choose?
How can they reduce the risks?

5. Describe the safety and the risks of a route you use.
How can you keep safe when you use this route?

What can you do to reduce risks and act responsibly when playing outside?

33

You do not need to eat meat.

Use the Internet.

Your diet should include meat.

A

Many people worry that when they stop eating meat and fish they might be in danger of some nutritional deficiency. This is not the case, as all the nutrients you need can easily be obtained from a vegetarian diet. In fact, research shows that, in many ways, a vegetarian diet is healthier than that of a typical meat-eater.

Iron is important in helping the blood take oxygen to all parts of the body. Iron deficiency can cause anaemia. It is the most common mineral nutritional deficiency in the world.

It is particularly important that teenage girls ensure they have enough iron. Iron is needed for red blood cells. It is found in leafy green vegetables, wholemeal bread, molasses, eggs, dried fruits , lentils and pulses. Vegetable sources of iron are not as easily absorbed as animal sources but, with plenty of vitamin C, this can be improved.

However, according to research, vegetarians are no more likely to suffer iron deficiency than
non-vegetarians.

From *Information Sheets: Basic Nutrition and Iron* (the Vegetarian Society UK 10.12.99)

You can read the whole of this report on **www.vegsoc.org**

B

Iron deficiency is the most commonly reported nutritional disorder during early childhood.

One in five of all children between the ages of $1\frac{1}{2}$ and $4\frac{1}{2}$ years is iron deficient.

We obtain our nutrients from a variety of foods and no single food can provide all we need.

Red meat is one of the best food sources of easily absorbed iron.

The iron in red meat is more easily absorbed than iron in fruit, vegetables, cereals and eggs.

Meat will also help the absorption of vegetables and cereals when eaten at the same meal.

Sources of iron easily absorbed: beef, lamb, pork, chicken, turkey, game, liver, kidney, oily fish, bacon, ham and meat products.

Sources of iron less easily absorbed: bread, fortified breakfast cereals, dried fruit (e.g. apricots), eggs, dark green vegetables, peas, beans, lentils, chocolate and cocoa.

From *British Meat: Meat and Iron* (Meat & Livestock Commission 1.12.99)

You can read the whole of this report on **www.meatmatters.com**

1. With a partner, read the reports on page 34.

List the facts given in each report.

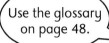
Use the glossary on page 48.

Facts are data from observations, investigations and surveys.

Facts	
Report A	**Report B**
Iron deficiency is the most common mineral nutritional deficiency in the world.	One in five of all children between the ages of $1\frac{1}{2}$ and $4\frac{1}{2}$ is iron deficient.

2. Explain why each report has these facts.

Copy and complete the table.

3. What is each report trying to say?

4. What are your views about a healthy diet?

Opinions are people's views about issues.

List some facts to support your views.

Use reference books.

Use CD-ROMs and the Internet.

Emergency

This is what happens during fire practice at one school.

1. From the pictures, work out what the fire procedure is at this school.
   Write the procedure as a set of rules.

Think about the order in which the rules are written.

2. Compare this fire procedure with that of your school.

   List the things you should do.
   List the things you should not do.

   Explain why.

3. With a partner, discuss your school's fire procedure.
Make a note of any questions you have about it.

4. In your group, make up a play to explain your school's fire procedure to the youngest children.

5. Find out about the fire procedures in other buildings.

What similarities are there among all fire procedures?

You could use a database or table to organise your findings.

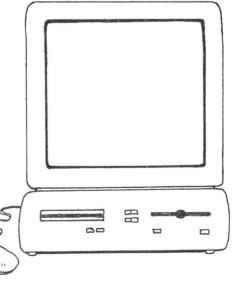

Prejudice

Sometimes people from different communities, cultures or religious faiths do not understand one another's way of life.

1. In a group, discuss what is happening in each picture.
   How do the people misunderstand one another?

2. Sometimes, prejudice makes us judge people without understanding.
   What might happen because of the prejudice in these pictures?

   Copy and complete the table.

Picture	Prejudice	Consequences
a		

3. List some differences between people that might cause prejudice or misunderstandings.

4. List some of the ways in which people are similar.

Think about homes, food, family, leisure activities, clothes and language.

Find out the exact meaning of **prejudice** and **discrimination**.

5. With a group, discuss why people may be prejudiced towards others. Why might they discriminate against others?

Copy and complete the table. List other people who may be treated unfairly.

People	Who might show prejudice towards them?	Why?	What is the effect on people?
old people			
children			
people with disabilities			
girls or women			
boys or men			
people from different cultures			

6. With a group, plan and enact a short play that shows people suffering because of prejudice or discrimination. The planning table may help.

7. Rewrite and enact the play with an ending that makes everyone happier.

Plan for a play

Characters	Scenes	
	Places	What happens

Useful materials

What can we all do to respect and understand one another better?

Jonathan had an accident when he was small.
As a result, he walks with a limp.
Sometimes other children make fun of him.

1. In a group, consider the scene in the picture.
How are Jed, Mark and Sharon being unkind to Jonathan?

Why do you think they walk behind him?
How might Jonathan feel?

2. How do you think the three children feel when they are making fun of Jonathan?

clever?

silly?

proud?

guilty?

42

Do you think they would do this if they were alone and not in a group?
How can David help Jonathan?
What can Jonathan do?

3. What do you think of the way Jed, Mark and Sharon behave?
Imagine you were with them when they were behaving like this.
What would you have done?

4. If Jed, Mark and Sharon were asked why they do this, they might say:

We're only teasing.

It's just a bit of fun.

We didn't mean any harm.

What would you say in reply?

5. Think of other ways in which people are teased or made fun of.

How they look.

How they dress.

How they speak.

Suggest ways they could deal with it.
How could people be encouraged to consider the feelings of others?

If someone was teasing or making fun of another person, what could you do?

John has noticed that his mum has been acting differently lately. Then he hears this conversation.

They'll be announcing who'll be made redundant any day. I don't know what we'll do.

Lindsay's dad had been waiting for the results of his exams for his new job.

Well, that's it. I'll never get the promotion now.

1. Sometimes we can see signs that show us how someone is feeling.

What might John have noticed about his mum recently?

How might Lindsay's dad have been showing his feelings?

2. How could the children act sensitively and help their parents cope?

> John could ...
>
> Lindsay could ...

There might be the things they don't do as well as those they do.

In these situations, we can guess how the people feel. We might base this on how we would feel ourselves.

But, another person's feelings about something may be very different from our own.

3. How sensitive are these children being to other people's feelings?

People can belong to many groups or communities.

1. List the groups or communities to which Catherine belongs.

2. To what groups or communities do you belong?

Make a list and compare your list with Catherine's.

Compare it with those of others in your class.

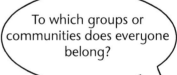
To which groups or communities does everyone belong?

We choose to belong to some groups.
We belong to others without choosing.

Who chooses where you are born, where you live and the school you go to?

3. Which groups from your list did you choose to belong to? Highlight them on your list.

4. Why did you choose to join these groups? What is good about being a member?

5. List some groups you might belong to in the future.

Your city, town or village is a community.

6. Draw and describe a special feature of where you live.

Chesterfield has a church with a crooked spire.

Think about places, people, industries, sports teams, buildings, visitors, and famous people who have lived there.

List the things that are special about your city, town or village.

Glossary

absorbed (34) — Soaked up.

anaemia (34) — A **deficiency** of red blood corpuscles.

antisocial (14) — Causing offence or harm to other people.

debate (23) — To discuss something, often in a public meeting.

deficiency (34) — If you have a deficiency of something, you do not have enough of it: for example, an important **mineral** such as iron.

discrimination (41) — Treating people unfairly because they belong to a particular group.

drug (29) — A material used as a medicine to cure or prevent illness or as a painkiller. A substance that some people take to alter their state of mind.

hygiene (26) — Cleanliness (being clean).

manifesto (23) — The beliefs and aims of a political party.

media (35) — All forms of communication between large groups of people (e.g. newspapers, television, the Internet).

mineral (34) — A material such as calcium, iron or sodium that the body needs in order to make the best use of food, which helps the body to function properly.

nicotine (29) — A poisonous substance in tobacco; it comes from the tobacco plant, nicotiana.

nutritional (34) — Concerning food.

personal qualities (2, 3, 22) — People's characteristics: for example, kindness, sense of humour or honesty.

prejudice (40) — Dislike for things or some people without understanding or knowing them.

procedure (36) — A set of instructions or ways of behaving in situations: for example, a fire procedure sets out what to do if there is a fire in a building.

puberty (10) — The time when the reproductive organs become mature (able to produce babies).

resolution (4, 5) — Something that someone makes up his or her mind to do.

respect (41) — Recognising people's right to fair treatment and to voice their opinion; valuing people.

responsibility (7, 16, 18) — An action or way of behaving that is important for a person to carry out. If you are responsible for something you are in charge of it or of doing it.

rule (36) — A statement about what must, or must not, be done.

sensitive (45) — Considering how other people feel; to avoid saying or doing things that will be hurtful or upsetting to them.

vegetarian (34) — Eating no meat or fish.

Other titles in this series:

Citizenship and PSHE Big Book A	9780007436941
Citizenship and PSHE Big Book B	9780007436958
Citizenship and PSHE Big Book C	9780007436965
Citizenship and PSHE Teacher Guide A	9780007436866
Citizenship and PSHE Teacher Guide B	9780007437368
Citizenship and PSHE Teacher Guide C	9780007436873
Citizenship and PSHE Book 1	9780007436903
Citizenship and PSHE Book 2	9780007436934
Citizenship and PSHE Book 3	9780007436842
Citizenship and PSHE Book 4	9780007436859
Citizenship and PSHE Teacher Guide 1	9780007436910
Citizenship and PSHE Teacher Guide 2	9780007436927
Citizenship and PSHE Teacher Guide 3	9780007437177
Citizenship and PSHE Teacher Guide 4	9780007437252

Published by Collins
An imprint of HarperCollinsPublishers
The News Building
1 London Bridge Street
London
SE1 9GF

HarperCollins Publishers
Macken House,
39/40 Mayor Street Upper,
Dublin 1,
D01 C9W8
Ireland

**Browse the complete Collins catalogue at
www.collins.co.uk**

© HarperCollinsPublishers Limited 2011, on behalf of the authors.
First published in 2000 by Folens Limited.

15

ISBN-13: 978-0-00-743684-2

Deena Haydon, Pat King and Christine Moorcroft assert their moral right to be identified as the authors of this work.

British Library Cataloguing in Publication Data
A catalogue record for this publication is available from the British Library.

Every effort has been made to trace copyright holders and to obtain their permission for the use of copyright material. The authors and publishers will gladly receive any information enabling them to rectify any error or omission in subsequent editions.

Editor: Alison MacTier
Layout artist: Patricia Hollingswroth
Cover design: Martin Cross
Illustrations: Jane Bottomley

Photographs
Page 23 (photos a and b) Luton Borough Council.
Page 23 (photo c) David Ball, The Stock Market.
Page 28 (all), 30 (all), 33 (both), 47 Christine Moorcroft.

Text
Page 34: Text reproduced by permission of the
Vegetarian Society and the Meat and Livestock Commission.

Printed and bound in the UK using 100% Renewable Electricity at CPI Group (UK) Ltd

This book is produced from independently certified FSC™ paper
to ensure responsible forest management.

For more information visit: www.harpercollins.co.uk/green